PINK
PURPOSE

Reneë Beck

PINK PURPOSE

Confident Femininity on the Pathway to Purpose

INSPIRED
PUBLISHING

Pink Purpose

Confident Femininity on the Pathway to Purpose

First Edition, First Impression 2021

ISBN 978-0-620-91146-7

Copyright © Reneë Beck

Published by:

Inspired Publishing

PO Box 82058 | Southdale | 2135

Johannesburg , South Africa

Email: info@inspiredpublishing.co.za

www.inspiredpublishing.co.za

"God will make this happen, for He who calls you is faithful."

1 Thessalonians 5:24

Purpose: [noun]

the reason for which something is done or created or for which something exists.

a person's sense of resolve or determination.

Raison d'être [French]: the reason for being

CONTENTS

DEDICATION

This book that you hold in your hands is a product of God's grace. He has wrapped me in it, covered me with it and reminded me of it at every turn. And for that I am forever grateful. Todah Abba!

IN LOVING MEMORY

This work is shared in memory of my paternal grandmother, Granny Jane Richardson. I am a product of those who went before me. Brave women like her who spoke life over me from the moment I came into the world. Today, I see the fruit of the words she spoke over me. They have chartered the pathway of my life and for that I am grateful.

It is also in memory of my Mother-In-Love, Beatrice Beck (Mommy Bea). A woman who always reminded me to keep my eyes fixed on Jesus. That in the midst of the storms of life all I need to do is to hold on to the hem of His garment and I will make it through. Our tea time chats will be forever embedded as a special memory in my heart.

ACKNOWLEDGEMENTS

My greatest gratitude:

To my Heavenly Father. Abba, thank You for allowing me the honour of being the carrier of this message. My greatest privilege in life is to be known as Your daughter.

To my Lord and Savior, Jesus Christ. Thank you, Lord, for dying for me, saving me and for being the way, truth and life. I treasure our relationship and the opportunity to tell others of Your saving grace. Forever, You're my King!

Thank you, dear Holy Spirit, for being with me every step of this journey. You have inspired me in the most incredible way and this book is the finished product of a journey we started together. To God be the glory, great things He has done!

To the love of my life, Hein. You are a reflection of God's grace towards me. You never seem to tire of hearing me speak about the things that I am passionate about. Thank you for giving me room to flourish and to pursue all that God has called me to.

You are the epitome of a loving and supportive husband and I wouldn't be able to do half of the things I do if it wasn't for you. You are now and forever my purpose partner and for that I am truly grateful.

To my parents, Mike & Liz Richardson, thank you for introducing me to Jesus. You have always been supportive of everything I do and want to do (now and in the future) and are always encouraging me to keep going. You constantly remind me to believe that the sky is not the limit and to constantly move forward one step at a time. My spirit of determination, work ethic and service to others as well as entrepreneurship come from you both and your ongoing wisdom, love and support made me who I am today.

To my Father-In-Love, my "Oom D" and Aunty Lorraine. Thank you for believing in my capabilities and always encouraging me to do what is in my heart to do. Your words of wisdom and constant prayer lift me up and keep me going, I appreciate you both so very much.

To my incredible siblings: Keith, Craig, Curtis, Keagan, Corlia, Sonja, Rudi & Joanne. A wonderful mix of the family of my birth and the family of my heart. The Richardsons and the Becks! You guys keep me smiling. You remind me to laugh, to keep singing, to keep going and to never give up. You have cheered me on in the most amazing ways and for that I am incredibly thankful.

To my niece, Zana: I hope this book will be a guide for you as you grow into all that God has for you. May you never forget that you are precious in the sight of the Lord, you are fearfully and wonderfully made, and that you have purpose.

To my nephews, Joshua and Ezra: Being your Aunty gives me great joy. May you both continue to grow up in the way of the Lord and never depart from it. May honour encompass your lives. I am nuts about you!

To the women in my family: Those who have gone before me and those who come after me, I am honoured to be a part of your bloodline. Thank you for inspiring me to believe bigger. May we never forget that brave women run in our family and bold women are a part of our blood.

To my purpose sisters: I want to acknowledge and say thank you to the women who have cheered me on and set me up to win. What started off as friendship has become true sisterhood. You are my sisters and I am thankful for our precious relationships. Each one of you are one of life's greatest blessings. I appreciate you.

To Pastor Willie Norris: I am incredibly blessed to have your contribution in this book. I am grateful for your vision, encouraged by your integrity and blessed to call you my Pastor. May the Lord richly bless you as you continue to make a contribution to not only my life, but to the lives of many.

To Darren and the Inspired Publishing Team: I am incredibly thankful that God allowed me the opportunity to partner with you in this important work. Thank you for your direction, input, wisdom and for helping me bring this vision to life.

FOREWORD

As Reneë's spiritual father and pastor, I am extremely privileged to write the foreword of her book. I am of the opinion that what I'm writing reflects my genuine opinion and interpretation of her book and in particular her personal life and character.

As I was reading the manuscript, I had this sense of so much gratitude to have Reneë as my spiritual daughter. I am not surprised that she wrote this book because she is a go-getter. She is someone who always does things in an excellent manner. This book is a reflection of her excellency in doing things. What you read in this book is not fabricated to promote the sales of the book. It is rather a portrayal of a person whose desire is to inspire other people by showing and being an example and doing justice by being a role model.

This book is written in a simple and understandable manner so that all can understand it, yet, it is based on a solid foundation of her belief and faith in Jesus Christ! The reader can, with ease, follow her teachings, guidance and inspiration for personal benefit.

Her honesty and approach in using herself as an example must be seen in the light as her desire to bring out everything within her to equip and be a blessing to the reader.

I trust many will read this book and find it as real talk for the times we live in.

I know God's blessing is on this book and I also bless Renëe and the book.

May the Lord bless you!

Pastor Willie Norris

Senior pastor: Gospel Workers Ministries

INTRODUCTION

"For I know the plans and thoughts that I have for you, says the Lord, plans for peace and well-being and not for disaster, to give you a future and a hope." Jeremiah 29:11

I don't know what my purpose is!

At some stage or another we have all found ourselves saying these exact words.

Or how about hearing for maybe the hundredth time that you were created on purpose, with purpose, for purpose. But what does it really mean?

Simply put, purpose is a reason for being and to understand that reason, we need to go back to the beginning, to God's original intent for creating you.

Believe me there is a reason you are here on this earth. Maybe you are yet to figure it out, or maybe you are on the journey but want to make sure you are on the right track. Whatever that looks like for you, there is one thing you must remember... Purpose has always been inside of you.

The truth is that God created each of us uniquely and in that uniqueness, lies the natural impact that you are supposed to have on the world. It's who you were meant to be before anyone else told you who you should be.

So, the story goes something like this: You were born, you started to grow and develop and there were things that you did without anybody teaching or directing you. These are the things that came naturally and without any prompting. Maybe you loved to dance, even if your rhythm was a little off, or you had an enquiring mind and loved to constantly ask a million questions that sometimes drove others to frustration. Perhaps you spent hours sitting and dreaming and allowing your imagination to take you places you hadn't yet seen.

And then what happened? You were labelled. You heard words like too talkative, a busy body, a day dreamer, and many other things. Those labels became the compass that directed your life and as you got older, you tried to do less of the thing that you got in trouble for. Over time, your light went dim and in many cases, your light died out completely.

The subject of purpose has literally paralyzed many women. We go around looking and trying to find our purpose thinking it is as elusive as finding a unicorn when in reality our purpose was never in hiding, we just never realized it for what it was.

We tend to discount our purpose because it doesn't appear in the packaging we imagined. Instead of stepping into our purpose and allowing God to guide us into it, we avoid, deny and even ignore it. What we forget is that our purpose comes from the way in which God has designed us. It lies in the presence our lives are meant to have on others, and it gives our lives significance. The moment we discover what that is, we will be well equipped to fulfil a unique purpose within the greater plan for humanity.

You have been given the gift of life for a reason. The moment you understand who you are, who God has created you to be and what you have living in the inside of you, you will be unstoppable. But let's get something straight. Purpose is NOT going to appear one day and say:

"Hey, here I am. Let's go and make an impact."

It's going to take digging deep, becoming more self-aware, doing the work and committing to living intentionally.

My goal in writing this book stems from my own journey and ultimate awakening to my own purpose. See it as your empowerment guide. Read it cover to cover and keep a notebook close by so you can write down notes or nuggets that bring you revelation.

I wrote this book to serve you and empower you to dream more, live bolder and believe bigger. I will share stories from my own experiences, give you moments to pause and reflect and provide you with tools to move forward.

You may well find that even as you read it, there will be a voice that tells you all the reasons you cannot dare to dream more, live bolder and believe bigger. It will say things like:

"You are not capable." and "Who do you think you are?"

In those moments, you get to choose: Listen to that voice and stop, or do it anyway.

The truth is, you no longer have the luxury of being stuck and that's why I wrote this book for you. To let you know that there is more for you to do. More than you ever thought possible.

You truly were created on purpose, with purpose, for purpose for such a time as this.

Know that I believe in you, I'm praying for you and I know that you can be all that God has created you to be.

Let's get to it!

CHAPTER 1

IDENTITY

CHAPTER 1

IDENTITY

THIS IS WHO I AM

"For You formed my innermost parts; You knit me [together]
in my mother's womb. I will give thanks and praise to You,
for I am fearfully and wonderfully made; Wonderful are Your
works, and my soul knows it very well. My frame was not
hidden from You, when I was being formed in secret, and
intricately and skillfully formed [as if embroidered with many
colors] in the depth of the earth. Your eyes have seen my
unformed substance; and in Your book, were all written the
days that were appointed for me, when as yet there was not
one of them [even taking shape]"

Psalms 139: 13-16

CHILDHOOD WONDER

If you were to ask my mother for two words to describe me, she would call me confident and brave. According to her, I was born with those two characteristics already being a part of me, but believe me, it wasn't always the case.

I grew up in the '80s, in a community where the colour of your skin and the texture of your hair was the standard of beauty by which you were measured. It dictated the way people responded to you and your level of importance in an unseen hierarchy.

As a little girl, I could never understand why was I the one to look different. My cousins, who I spent my childhood with, were extremely light skinned with straight, long, beautiful hair that you could run your fingers through. The picture of what it meant to not only be beautiful but to be accepted.

I also had a family member who incessantly teased me about having a big forehead and although in hindsight I see it as the teasing of a young boy, at the time, there was nothing funny about it. I didn't see it at first, but the more I heard it, the more I believed it.

I can remember getting home from school one day, after being teased by an older boy who decided that the name "Black Cat" was a fitting description of how he saw me. That day, as I stared at myself in the mirror, tears rolled down my face and I wondered how I could make myself look different.

What I could do to change the way I looked so that I could be more acceptable to the people who had placed a label on me.

Something you need to know is that I grew up in a home with two loving parents who always affirmed me. My mom has always been my greatest support and she constantly reminded me how special I was and that God loved me. She spoke life into me.

But on this day, staring into the mirror I didn't believe it. I felt that somehow God had made a mistake. I cried and cried because there was nothing I liked about the way I looked. I was disappointed in the picture that was looking back at me. On that day, through the negative experience brought about by that bullying boy, two things happened. Firstly, I decided that no one was ever going to make me feel less-than ever again, and also, that I would stand up for myself against anyone who dared to come at me.

So, while staring at a face I wished I could change, I discovered the powerful concept of self-talk. I'm not really sure why I said it out loud, maybe because it seemed to be an important moment, but I said:

"Reneë, there is no room for tears. You need to toughen up, and don't let anyone bring you down."

The second thing that happened was that I stopped enjoying looking at myself in the mirror and began to hate taking photos. I dreaded having my photo taken because I never wanted to see the image it portrayed. Whether it was for a family outing or for school photo day, I would literally freeze and want to climb out of my skin. Actually, it became one of the biggest reasons my mother and I got into arguments because she believed in capturing moments and I believed in not wanting to capture my face forever.

IMAGINING MYSELF CONFIDENT

My childhood was, what many people would call, idyllic. My parents showered me and my brothers with love, care and attention. They made sure that I knew how important I was to them. Unfortunately, my identity and self-worth were being narrated by external influences and it caused me to create an identity that worked for me. This identity wouldn't allow anyone to walk all over me, it did everything to not stand out too much, was not sentimental and believed I could quickly move on from any crisis. One who built relationships but was hesitant for people to get too close for fear of being reliant on them. I rarely asked for help and believed that if I was just tough, I could handle anything that came my way. What started out as confidence quickly became a crutch that I proudly carried like a badge and in the process, my heart became hardened, I lacked empathy and I believed that no one could get to me. Sure, I was strong, but my confidence came from the wrong place.

You see, our identity is established long before we were even in our mother's wombs. Genesis 1:27 says: "So God created man in His own image, in the image of God He created him; male and female He created them."

This means that what we would look like was already established long before we were in our mother's wombs.

God already knew. He knew how you would look and why you would look the way you did. He already knew who you were meant to be. Unfortunately, the world distorts that view. Along the journey of life, that image gets corrupted by the way people treat us and by the things they say to us. It shapes us into what it sees as acceptable, worthy or significant.

It paints for us a picture of how we could look better and be better so that our identity gets wrapped up in who they say we are, as opposed to who God created us to be. It begins to dictate how we see ourselves, the things we do, the relationships we pursue and the path we follow in life. It becomes the badge we wear as validation. We feel that this is who we are because of what "they" told us.

In an age of social media it seems that now, more than ever, at every turn we are getting messages constantly trying to tell us who we are. That we are not good enough as we are, that we should strive for bigger and better no matter the fallout.

So, how do we discover what our true identity is?

FEARFULLY AND WONDERFULLY MADE

I was 19 years old, happily going through my teens as only a teen girl can, but I felt like something was missing. A friend of my parents came to visit one day and before she was about to leave she asked to speak to me. I was very surprised because I didn't know her very well and couldn't imagine what it was she had to say. I can still remember her words as if it was just the other day. She said,

"The Lord wants me to ask you a question. He wants to know if you know who you are."

Well, I burst into tears. Right there, in front of a relative stranger, I balled my eyes out. It was a question I had been asking myself for a long time and to hear someone else say it out loud shook me. She told me to read Psalms 139:13-16 because God wanted me to remember that I am His, that I am His image bearer and that He had made me fearfully and wonderfully. This was a turning point for me. I began to read scripture that spoke to who my Creator was and who He had created me to be.

Labels take away your value and limit your potential. They replace your true identity in Christ with false identities. When you allow the labels of others to define who you are, you function in the confines of that label. Your true image gets distorted by the opinions of others, and you begin to answer to their perceived image of you. You are only who or what you answer to and who you are is not what you have done or what was done to you. When you begin to understand and embrace who God has called you to be, you will not answer to anything less. You will remember that He calls you daughter, His beloved, His workmanship, made in His image.

It is time for you to rise up, to cast off the labels, to discover your identity and walk in the plan and purpose that God has for your life.

I have tried and tested a few things, but these are the things that helped me:

- As a teenager, I discovered a scripture that became my power declaration. I would quote it over and over again as a reminder of who I really was at my core. This is something I still do today.

- I learnt how to shut off the negative words that went against what I believed to be true.

- I began to journal consistently. I have always loved words and this is my outlet to get clarity and focus.

- I became very careful of who I spent my time with. I didn't always get it right but I became very aware of who I allowed to speak into my life and be an influence.

My own journey developed in me a resilient attitude, a sense of confidence and an ability to embrace who I am; flaws and all. The thing is that in order to fulfill your purpose, you must first know and celebrate who you are.

What do you want your journey to teach you?

_____

_____

_____

LET'S PAUSE AND REFLECT HERE

_____

PURPOSE QUESTIONS:

Before you imagine this big overhaul, I want you to think about some of the things people have said that caused you to question who you are.

Now ask yourself:

- Is it true?

- Who am I at my core?

- Who did God create me to be?

- How do I want to be remembered?

Because of a journey that started out as a little girl, today I can confidently answer these questions without hesitation. How about you? Take the time to pause, reflect and write down your responses.

This will be your first step in your own journey of discovery.

PURPOSE ACTION:
Write down 3 things you love about yourself.

1._____

2. _____

3._____

CHAPTER 2

GIFTS & TALENTS

CHAPTER 2

GIFTS & TALENTS
YOUR SUPERPOWERS

"Since we have gifts that differ according to the grace given to us, each of us is to use them accordingly: if [someone has the gift of] prophecy,]let him speak a new message from God to His people] in proportion to the faith possessed; if service, in the act of serving; or he who teaches, in the act of teaching; ore he who encourages, in the act of encouragement, he who gives, with generosity; he who leads, with diligence; he who shows mercy [in caring for others], with cheerfulness.

Romans 12:6-8

WHAT'S IN YOUR HANDS

Now that we have gone through the journey of discovering who you at your core, let's talk about gifts and talents, or as I like to call them - your superpowers.

What exactly is a gift and talent and how do I know what mine is? That is a great question!

Your gift or talent is that thing that comes naturally to you. Something you were born with. You didn't have to go to school for it, you didn't have someone teach you how to do it because it was always just a part of who you are. Your gift or talent is what God specifically deposited into you when He made you. They are a part of your spiritual DNA and exclusively inside you.

Growing up, our house was always filled with music. I remember so many moments sitting with my two brothers and parents while my dad played the guitar and we would sing songs. My brothers and I had a natural talent for singing. So much so that wherever we went we would be asked to sing. We would spend time rehearsing and putting together a stage act for whenever we had the opportunity to sing, whether it be at a church worship evening, family event or even just during our road trips. Singing came naturally to us from a very young age and it was something we enjoyed doing. A talent for singing led to us learning to play instruments and joining the school choir. We nurtured the talent and it became an area we were gifted in. This talent for singing turned us into worshippers.

The older I got, the more this talent manifested in me writing songs and poetry. I also discovered another gift that was not as well received. I loved to talk! I always found myself asking numerous questions, wanting to know why things were the way they were and I also enjoyed the process of sharing new information.

Because of my love for words and expressing myself in this way, I was given the label of "she talks too much" and "miss know-it-all". After hearing those labels enough times, I decided that I would talk less. I wouldn't express myself so boldly, and so, I buried my gift of communication for a very long time. As a result, I disliked anything to do with speaking in public. I was okay with being on stage and singing with my brothers, but when it came to doing anything on my own and using my voice for it, I shrank away.

There are things that you won't think of as a gift because you got into trouble for them. This is because when people don't understand the gift, they redirect it or even cause you to doubt it. Any gift you possess needs to be channeled in the right direction, it needs to be cultivated and nurtured in order for it to grow. If that doesn't happen, you go in circles and your gift is smothered.

You have been blessed with certain gifts and talents to use during your time here on earth. You have a duty to share the gifts you've been blessed with. There are people who need exactly what you have to offer, exactly how you offer it. Your unique DNA compels you to do exactly that.

Don't believe me?

There's a woman who, since 1996, has made her living as a cheese sculptor. Yes, you heard right – she sculpts cheese. Surely, there's room for you!

UNLOCKING TREASURE

I want you to imagine, if you will, a ring of keys, and as you hold this bunch of keys in your hand, you notice that they are all different sizes. But the most interesting thing about these keys is that each one is ornate and has a special design on them. This ring of keys fills your palm, extending beyond your fingertips on one end and beyond your wrist on the other. They are unlike any keys you have ever seen or used before and as you continue inspecting these keys you begin to imagine what treasure they could possibly unlock. That is when you notice something you didn't see at first - engraved on each key is your name. There is also an instruction label which says that you are to use these keys to unlock the treasures that are buried inside of you, that you will get an opportunity to use these keys at the right time and that they will lead you to your specific assignment and calling. All you have to do is choose, right now, before you do anything else, to receive these keys and take seriously the privilege of using them.

That is exactly how I want you to think of your gifts and talents. They have been specifically given to you for a reason. Your gifts will unlock closed doors.

So, how do you uncover your unique gifts, and use them to make an impact?

It's going to take more than just sitting and thinking about it, hoping that one day the epiphany will hit you over the head or that you will receive a personal invitation from someone.

The unfortunate truth is that most of us go through life completely missing our calling because we get caught up in the thinking instead of the doing. Of course, you need to take the time to reflect, but it's also going to require you to take intentional action.

It is through the intentional action that clarity comes and once you have the clarity, it will lead you to awakening to your purpose.

WHAT HELPED ME:

- I began to understand that the gifts and talents God gave me are specifically for me.

- I got direction on how to use my gifts and talents for impact.

- I became intentional about using my gifts and talents.

- I learnt to sow my gifts in the right places.

What you have makes you different from anyone else. It's time that you put some thought into what gives you your uniqueness. Once you are able to clearly define what your gifts and talents are, you will then have the clarity you need to move forward.

LET'S PAUSE AND REFLECT HERE

PURPOSE QUESTIONS:

- What do you enjoy doing most?

_____

_____

- What are the gifts you have doubted, dismissed or denied?

_____

_____

- What have you always wanted to do but have been afraid to attempt?

_____

_____

Never forget that your gift has to do with serving and helping people. Be a good steward of the resources that you have been entrusted with. Some people use their gifts to volunteer for projects that better their communities, eradicate diseases, employ the homeless, feed the hungry, give comfort to the struggling, or fight injustice in creative, unique and powerful ways. Whatever that looks like to you, uncovering your superpowers will cause you to make an impact in a significant way.

PURPOSE ACTION:

- Choose one gift and resolve to improve on it.

CHAPTER 3

PASSION

CHAPTER 3

PASSION

WHAT SETS YOUR HEART ON FIRE?

"Every great dream begins with a dreamer. Always
remember, you have within you the strength, the patience,
and the passion to reach for the stars to change the world."
Harriet Tubman

BORN TO DREAM

Children think that they can do anything! They dream big dreams. If you ask a child what they want to be when they grow up, they will respond with confidence. You will get responses like: an Astronaut, the President, a Doctor, a Soccer player or whichever recording artist is popular at the time. The dreams of a child are seen through an unfiltered lens, but something happens as we grow older. We stop dreaming. We begin to see dreams as ridiculous, never going to happen, or for someone else, just not me. We settle for good enough. We settle for mediocre. We settle for complacency. We stifle the things we really want to do in the hopes that we will soon forget about it. We surrender our dreams under the banner of "maturity" and being practical. Phrases like these become our way of justifying why we just won't go for it:

- Don't get your hopes up; you'll just get disappointed.

- Be realistic, there are so many people already doing [fill in the blank].

- What's the point in dreaming about it, when it will never happen?

- I'm too old to consider doing that.

- I don't know enough to make it a success. And the list goes on…

Acknowledging your dreams can feel scary. It's so much better to stay in the comfort zone, to be practical, to not take the risk. So, you keep the dream to yourself, tuck it away, forgotten and unspoken, but have you actually thought of what would happen if you dared to dream?

What would happen if you just decided to go for it?

As you give yourself permission to dream again, to pick up the desires that have laid dormant in the corners of your heart, there are two things I want to encourage you to do:

- Speak up. Tell one person about the dream you have. There is great power in speaking things into existence. It will give you the encouragement you need and also create a deeper level of ownership and accountability for your dream.

- Put it on paper. As soon as you start to own your dream, fear will creep in again to tell you all the reasons you can't do it. Sometimes that voice of negativity gets really loud. You see, as long as your dream remains in the corners of your heart, it will stay dormant and unrealized. That's why you need to write it down.

According to Dr. Gail Matthews, psychology professor at Dominican University in California, you are 42 percent more likely to achieve it just by writing it down.

So, don't wait much longer it's time to treat your dreams as something of great value – because they are. As Seth Godin says, *"Own your dreams. There is no better way to make them happen."* But it all starts with owning them.

"It is pleasant to see dreams come true..." Proverbs 13:19

FOLLOW YOUR PASSION

How many times have you heard someone say: "Follow your passion and you will never work another day in your life." or "Follow your passion and the money will come." The idea behind this saying is that as long as you follow your passion, you are bound to be successful at it.

This is not true!

Passion is about the things that excite you. It energizes you in such a way that you don't mind working on it day and night because it fuels something inside of you. Passion makes you wake up very early in the morning and go to bed late because you love it. It's your thing!

Raise your hand if you know of any people who are following their passion and are not making any progress in life. They stay broke and yet continue year after year to follow their passion. It just hasn't manifested into much.

This is where you say: "But I have to be passionate about what I do." No argument there, but here's the thing: just because you are passionate about something and you enjoy doing it, doesn't mean it's what you were purposed to do. If it's not getting you to the place you need to be, then it's a hobby. It may be something you can dabble in during your spare time, but it may not be your life's purpose.

Some of us are highly passionate about things that we are not gifted in and the result is that we hold on and force our way into making it succeed. Have the wisdom to understand what your gifting is, because if you don't, you will spend time being passionate about things God did not gift you to do. Sometimes the problem isn't that things are not working out, the problem is that you are out of alignment.

I love to sing, like really love it, I can even go as far as to say I am passionate about music, but I understand that singing is not the direction I should take in using my voice. My voice needs to be used in the role of encourager, in speaking life over dormant dreams and propelling others into their destinies. That doesn't mean that on occasion I won't enjoy an opportunity to sing. It just means that I know that although I am passionate about singing, it is reserved for a certain event or project or even just singing around the house. It is not what God has called me to.

The risk we take in spending all our time focusing on the things we are passionate about is that the things we are truly purposed to do sit on the sidelines, while there are people waiting for you to walk into your purpose. What you have to grasp is that your passion serves you, your purpose serves other people.

Now, you may be wondering, how do I know the difference between my gift and my passion? You know that you are operating in passion when no one is calling you. No one calls me to sing at an event but people definitely call me to speak at an event.

The key is to become passionate about your gifts. The truth is that sometimes you are not passionate about your gift, so it is important to understand how to apply the gift to what you are passionate about.

For example, you may have the gift of communication – you are always asked to be the one to write in the retirement card, to say a few words at a family function or even help to draft a notice for a work announcement, but you are passionate about finance, you love to share ideas on how to effectively budget, where to shop for the best deals or how to incorporate goals into your financial plan. Here is what it would look like to merge your gift of communication with your passion for finance: You could do workshops on financial literacy, you could share tips and tricks to establish a habit of saving. You could even write a book on becoming financially savvy.

Whatever that may look like for you, you have the opportunity to walk in your gifting while doing something you are passionate about.

The next step is to figure out how you can help people with what you have to offer, because ultimately, your purpose is your gift, passion and calling coming together to be of service to others.

What is that dream you have in your heart? You know the one. I know that as you read those words, it crossed your mind like a whisper. What is the picture that you have for your life? Sometimes it's vivid, bold and sometimes it's scary but it's yours. Yours to imagine and yours to fulfill. Give yourself permission to dream again, to ignite the passion and pursue purpose.

Things that helped me:

- I literally blocked out time to sit and dream.

- I made a list of my superpowers (gifts and talents) and what I'm passionate about.

- I started a gratitude and dream planning journal. Every day I write the things I am grateful for and ten dreams I want to see happen.

- I prayed over everything and entrusted my dreams to my heavenly Father.

LET'S PAUSE AND REFLECT HERE

_____

PURPOSE QUESTIONS:

- What is that dream you have in your heart?

  _____

  _____

- What are you passionate about?

  _____

  _____

- Where do you have the greatest opportunity to serve others?

  _____

  _____

- What are the things that bring you joy?

  _____

  _____

"Never doubt God's mighty power to work in you and accomplish all this. He will achieve infinitely more than your greatest request, your most unbelievable dream, and exceed your wildest imagination! He will outdo them all, for His miraculous power constantly energizes you". Ephesians 3:20

How marvelous is it to know that even the things we dream about are nothing compared to what God has in mind for us?

I spent years talking myself out of my dreams. It was easier to cheer others on from the sidelines instead of giving myself a chance. That was until I had the audacity to believe that my dreams are worth pursuing too.

If God said He will outdo your biggest dream and exceed your imagination, that means that you have to give Him something to bless. You need to not only trust Him with your dreams, but you need to believe in them too.

It's your time, time to say YES to your dreams!

PURPOSE ACTION:

- Grant yourself the permission to dream. Write down the 10 dreams you want to see happen.

CHAPTER 4

MINDSET

CHAPTER 4

MINDSET

AS A WOMAN THINKETH SO IS SHE

"Our life is what our

thoughts make it."

Marcus Aurelius

WARRIOR THINKING

Let me ask you a question: What could you achieve if you just thought better of yourself? If you realized how powerful your thoughts are, you would never again think a negative thought.

The truth is that our thoughts, good or bad have an effect on our physical bodies. Science has proven that positive, hopeful thoughts increase energy, whereas negative, hopeless one's drain energy. In fact, research shows that 75 to 98 percent of mental, physical, and behavioral illness comes from one's thought life.

Your mind is a powerful thing, and your thoughts have the ability to affect your performance in every area of your life. In fact, your life cannot go forward if your mind is going backward!

A professional athlete is a great example of how to do this. He has developed the ability to think about the next successful play and not the unsuccessful one that he just had. He may examine his less-than- stellar performance in order to learn from it, but he doesn't have to wallow in the negativity of it.

Do you think about what you are thinking about? This may sound funny, however learning to regularly take inventory of our thoughts is essential to having a good life. Instead of being an "unthinking" person, you can train yourself to think about what's going on in your mind. Having a healthy mindset is not automatic. It is an intentional practice!

In the Bible, we read in Ephesians 4:23: "*and be continually renewed in the spirit of your mind [having a fresh, untarnished mental and spiritual attitude]*"

A transformed mind leads to transformed words, moods and attitudes. It leads to amazing results.

MARKED FOR GREATNESS

One of the most inspiring stories I have come across is that of Roger Bannister, the first athlete to break the 4-minute mile. According to legend, experts said for years that the human body was simply not capable of a 4-minute mile. It wasn't just dangerous, it was impossible. Added to that, there were stories of how people had tried for years to break the barrier, even going so far as to tie bulls behind them to increase the incentive to do the impossible.

In the 1940's, the mile record was pushed to 4:01, where it stood for nine years, as runners struggled with the idea that maybe the experts had it right. Perhaps the human body had reached its limit and was incapable of going any further.

And then a breakthrough came.

On May 6, 1954, Roger Bannister broke the 4-minute barrier, running the distance in 3:59.4. He became the first man ever to do so, breaking through a mystical barrier and creating an unforgettable moment in sports history. As part of his training, he relentlessly visualized the achievement in order to create a sense of certainty in his mind and body.

This feat became a symbol of human achievement, but the important point to focus on here is that it took a sense of extreme certainty for Roger Bannister to do what was considered undoable. He was able to create that certainty in himself without seeing any proof that it could be done.

The Chinese have a saying: "The man who says it cannot be done should not interrupt the man doing it."

At the end of the day it is your thinking that determines what you accomplish.

NEVERTHELESS, SHE PERSISTED

Cordia Harrington is famously known as the "Bun Lady," and she is the founder, CEO and President of the Tennessee Bun Company, the world's fastest high-speed baked goods company, producing one thousand buns per minute. She was named #16 of the 25 Top Women Business Builders by FAST Company in 2005, and she has received a long list of other awards and accolades over the years. But her idea to start a bun business wasn't an overnight success. She was rejected by McDonalds not once, not twice, but thirty-one times! Thirty-one times she "failed" but thirty-one times, she persisted. When asked why she didn't give up, she said, "No wasn't an option."

Cordia knew what she was trying to accomplish and so she never gave up. She decided on what she wanted to achieve and she persevered despite the many rejections. She continued passed the setbacks because she knew what her motivation was and she set her mind on accomplishing it.

Are you like Cordia, to keep persisting until you achieve what you set out to do, or would you have given up after seven or eight times? This speaks not only of resiliency but on setting your mind on something and accomplishing it.

The Bible says in Philippians 4:8: "Finally believers, whatever is true, whatever is honorable and worthy of respect, whatever is right and confirmed by God's word, whatever is pure and wholesome, whatever is lovely and brings peace, whatever is admirable and of good repute; if there is any excellence, if there is anything worthy of praise, think continually on these things [center your mind on them, and implant them in your heart]."

I think that this is the best measuring stick as you think about what you are thinking about. If it does not fall into any of those categories, then you shouldn't be thinking about it. To break through the limitations of your mind, you need to smash the lies that fill you with insecurity and diminish your confidence.

Thoughts are real, physical things that occupy mental real estate. Moment by moment, every day, you are changing the structure of your brain through your thinking. When we hope, it is an activity of the mind that changes the structure of our brain in a positive and normal direction.

You have the ability to essentially renew your mind. We control our brain through our thinking and choosing. Although we cannot control the things that happen in our life, we can control our reactions to them.

Here are a few things that helped boost my confidence and establish a healthy mindset:

- I became mindful of how I think of myself. I remember that I am an image bearer of God, and I need to see myself the way He sees me.

- I affirm myself and speak words of life. I stick post-it notes with words of affirmations where I can easily see them.

- I quiet the inner critic. Some of the harshest comments come from our own mouths. I find opportunities to compliment, congratulate and even reward myself.

- It's hard to feel good about yourself if you are constantly bombarded with negativity. I take time out for soul care. I spend time in worship, reading the Bible and speaking with others who sharpen me with positive words.

LET'S PAUSE AND REFLECT HERE

PURPOSE QUESTIONS:

- Are you aware of what you are thinking about?

  _____

  _____

- How have your thoughts affected the way you see yourself?

  _____

  _____

- What are you telling yourself about your abilities?

  _____

  _____

PURPOSE ACTION:

- Grab a notebook and pen, take a few breaths, set a timer for three minutes and write down the negative messages you hear in your head that allow doubt to creep in.

- Now replace those negative messages with positive ones.

Your mindset is the blueprint for success in life. If you don't have the right mindset, nothing is possible, but with the right mindset, you can achieve great things.

You are responsible for every result in life. If you want different results you have to change your thoughts and actions.

"Once your mindset changes, everything on the outside will change along with it." Steve Maraboli

CHAPTER 5

PURPOSE KILLERS

CHAPTER 5

PURPOSE KILLERS

IDENTIFYING DESTINY DESTROYERS

"But whatever you do, find the God-centered, Christ-exalting, Bible-saturated passion of your life, and find your way to say it and live it and die for it. And you will make a difference that lasts. You will not waste your life."

John Piper

No one wants to be a loser yet so many of us live in quiet desperation, with a yearning and a longing to be and do more. Somehow we fail to fulfil our dream and walk in purpose. In this chapter, we will discuss what I call the purpose killers. Those things that stand in the way of, or even have the potential to destroy, your path to purpose.

These may look different to each of us, but there are common ones which we will go through.

PURPOSE KILLER #1: DISTRACTION

Have you heard of Shiny Object Syndrome (SOS)? At its core, shiny object syndrome is a disease of distraction. When SOS sets in, it forces you to chase project after project, and change after change, never settling for one option. The reason it's called shiny object syndrome is because it's the adult equivalent of a small child chasing after shiny objects. Once the child reaches the shiny object and sees what it is, they immediately lose interest and start chasing the next thing.

Wanting to investigate new opportunities is not inherently a bad goal, however, when SOS becomes rampant you run the risk of experiencing some serious setbacks:

- Inability to finish projects
- Poor planning of your ideas
- Confusion
- Overwhelm

The truth is that if you chase two rabbits, both will escape.

I once heard a story of a lion tamer, who lived almost a century ago, named Clyde Beatty. He became famous for his "fighting act" in which he would tame fierce wild animals. At one point, Beatty's act included a segment where he brought lions, tigers, cougars and hyenas into the circus ring all at once and tamed the entire group. Can you just imagine the sight?

The interesting thing is that in an era where the majority of lion tamers died in the ring, Beatty lived into his 60s. In the end, it was cancer that ended his life, not a lion.

How did he manage to do this? By incorporating a simple idea. He was one of the first lion tamers to bring a chair into the circus ring.

Why is this important?

If you have a look at the classic image of a lion tamer, it's one where he's holding a whip and a chair. The whip holds the attention during the act but it's mostly for show. It is the chair that does the important work. When a lion tamer would hold a chair in front of the lion's face, the lion tried to focus on all four legs of the chair at the same time. This caused the lion's focus to be divided because it becomes confused and unsure about what to do next. When faced with so many options, the lion chooses to freeze and wait instead of attacking the man holding the chair.

How often do you find yourself in the same position as the lion? You have something you want to achieve, you set out to do it only to end up confused by all of the options in front of you and you never make progress.

The Bible says that being double-minded makes you unstable and restless in all your ways, in everything you think, feel or decide. If you have a split focus, it will lead you to taking less action, making less progress and staying the same when you could be improving.

HOW TO OVERCOME IT:

- Set both short and long-term goals.
- Choose and commit to one specific task.
- Decide to become intentional about your goals.
- Abandon unnecessary projects.
- Manage your time well.

PURPOSE KILLER #2: PEOPLE PLEASING

This is a big one and my advice is, stop waiting for others to validate you! If you are going to wait on someone to give you the green light before you use your gifts and talents, or realize your dream, you will be waiting a very long time.

There has to come a point in your life where you decide who you are going to be. It's time for you to figure out what you really want. Not what your grandmother, or sister, or spouse wants. What do you want? Have you taken the time to sit and really figure it out, or have you been riding the wave of uncertainty as you get tossed to and fro between the ideas of others?

Well my friend, let this be your wakeup call!

Are you going to be a pleaser or are you going to be a producer?

HOW TO KNOW IF YOU ARE A PEOPLE PLEASER:

- You pretend to agree with everyone.
- You take responsibility for how others feel.
- You apologize often.
- You can't say no.
- You change your behavior based on who you are around.
- You constantly need praise and for people to affirm you.
- You go to great lengths to avoid conflict.

There is a scripture that has always stood out to me. Whenever I am weighing up my reasons for doing something,

I test it against this verse in Galatians 1:10: *"Am I now trying to win the favor and approval of men, or of God? Or am I seeking to please someone? If I were still trying to be popular with men, I would not be a bond- servant of Christ."*

You should only seek to please God in all that you do. The moment you seek to please others is the moment you miss out on being everything that God has called you to be.

I want you to understand this truth: You do not have the power to make others happy! No one does.

You will never walk in your purpose if you are constantly trying to be everything to everyone. Not only will it wear you out, it will lead you to a place of discouragement and a discouraged person is a purposeless person.

It's time to put an end to people pleasing. Walk in your purpose and have freedom. It is not anyone's place to validate that purpose. Life is about purpose not popularity.

HOW TO OVERCOME IT:

- Become self-aware.
- Realize you have a choice and can set your own expectations.
- Learn to say "No" with conviction.
- Set boundaries.

PURPOSE KILLER #3: FEAR

"One of the most common causes of failure is the habit of quitting when one is overtaken by temporary defeat".
Napoleon Hill

I once heard a story of a village where the children were told by their parents:

"Whatever you do, don't go near the top of the mountain. It's where the monster lives."

All the previous generations of children heeded this warning and avoided going near the top of the mountain.

One day, some brave young men in the village decided that they had to go and see the monster for themselves. They wanted to see what it was really like and defeat it. So, they loaded their packs with provisions and set off up the mountain. Halfway up, they were stopped in their tracks by a huge roar and a terrible stench. Half the men ran down the mountain, screaming in fear. The other half of the group continued on their journey. As they got farther up the mountain, they noticed that the monster was smaller than they had expected – but it continued to roar and emit such a stench that all but one of the men ran back down the mountain back to the village.

"I am going to get the monster."

The one remaining man said this to himself, and he took another step forward. As he did so, the monster shrank until it was the same size as the man. As he took another step towards the monster, it shrank again. It was still hideously ugly and continued to emit the stench, but the man was so close to the monster now that he could actually pick it up and hold it in the palm of his hand. As he looked at it, he said to the monster,

"Well then, who are you?"

In a tiny, high-pitched voice, the monster squeaked: "My name is fear."

This story gives such an accurate description of the way fear works. It seems so monstrous and horrible and scary until you begin to confront it and when you do, it becomes small enough to handle.

You know what? Fear is probably the greatest destructive force known to humanity. It breaks you down, destroys your confidence and may even paralyze you into inaction. Fear can be so paralyzing that it can render a person unable to jump from a burning building, even though the firemen with nets stand below to catch her.

Choosing to step outside that fear can be scary because it means things are going to change. We tend to like the familiar and this causes us to stay in our comfort zone, so by using fear as an excuse we sabotage our own success and remain where we are.

We often avoid making decisions out of fear of making a mistake. Actually, the failure to make decisions is one of life's biggest mistakes.

HOW TO OVERCOME IT:

- Fear is a limiting belief and it has more power in the battlefield of your mind. Instead, call your fears out by listing them.

- Read what the Bible says about overcoming fear. Mediate on scriptures that help you to focus on the truth.

- Embrace the unknown. Remind yourself that you have one life and God has big plans for you outside of your comfort zone.

- Walk in faith and be willing to take one step at a time, trusting that God is going to guide you all the way.

PURPOSE KILLER #4: LIVING IN TRAUMA

"When we are no longer able to change a situation, we are challenged to change ourselves." Victor Frankl

The question we ask when we have been though great trauma is: "Why me?" And this is what trauma does. It brings us to the place of questioning what we did wrong and how can we possibly change it. We replay different outcomes over and over in our mind and continue to relive the place of our trauma.

On the evening of September 24, 1942, Dr. Viktor Frankl kissed his wife as they both prepared to go to bed. This familiar gesture was one that they had repeated hundreds of times during their marriage. Little did he know that his life would change dramatically in a few short hours. In the early hours of the following morning, the Nazi army entered into his home and forced him and his family to leave, wearing nothing but their pajamas in the brutal cold of winter.

Dr. Frankl was immediately separated from his family. During the first few weeks of his imprisonment he was starved, beaten, and forced to walk from one concentration camp to another completely naked.

To "help" him never forget how close he was to death, the Nazi guards gave him the task of removing dead bodies from the camp or shoveling the charred remains and ashes out of the gas chambers. He spent three years in the concentration camps with days marked by uncertainty about whether he would be alive to see the next day.

His mind would drift to the warmth of his bed and the beauty of his wife and the laughter of his children in an effort to build a sense of sanity in the midst of incredible despair and chaos.

He had no idea that everyone he loved: his wife, children, parents and brother were all dead; some from the inhumane conditions of their concentration camps and others from the flame of gas ovens.

One day, while sitting alone and naked on a cement floor of his small cell, Dr. Frankl became aware of what he later called "the last of human freedoms." His Nazi captors could control his body, kill his friends and family, and make him do the most unthinkable acts for their pure entertainment, but Frankl discovered that in the midst of it all he still retained the power to choose how to be affected by it.

The power to choose how we respond is a power that can never be taken.

The thought of the suffering that Dr. Frankl had to endure is unimaginable. He lost everything: his loved ones, his possessions, his sense of control over his life and body. Yet, in the midst of deep evil and cruelty, he discovered that he had a choice in how he allowed these events to affect him. This in itself shows great strength of character and is a powerful awareness that can be of great value to us all.

Attempting to answer the question: "Why me?" means understanding a set of facts that you may never begin to grasp. Knowing why something happened doesn't change what happened. The important thing is how you move from a place of powerlessness to a position of power.

Like Dr. Frankl, we are faced with the challenge of looking at what happened to us and choosing how we respond to it going forward.

PURPOSE KILLER #5: COMPARISON

"Comparison is the thief of joy." Theodore Roosevelt

"A thoroughbred horse never looks at other horses, it just concentrates on running the fastest race it can." How true is this quote from Henry Ford?

If you are focusing on what the person next to you is doing, how will you ever run your own race?

Don't make the mistake of always comparing yourself to someone. In the process, you are rejecting and disapproving of the person God created you to be.

Think of having a beautifully wrapped gift presented to you. Without even opening the gift you decide to put it aside and ignore it. Imagine how God feels when you take the beautiful, free gift that He has given you, put it aside and chase something else, coveting others who use their own gifts as intended. What would it look like if you decided to pick up the gift, see what is inside and use what you have been given? The things that were specifically chosen for your benefit.

The thing is, the world is not a place of scarcity, it is a place of abundance. And in that abundance, we need to realize that there is place for every single one of us. There is a spot for you, wherever you choose to make it and celebrating and supporting someone else takes nothing away from you. In fact, it only makes you better.

How you know when you are constantly comparing yourself to others:

- You label yourself based on what you see in others.

- You are never pleased with anything you achieve.

- You think you are less than someone else.

"Make a careful exploration of who you are and the work you have been given, and then sink yourself into that. Don't be impressed with yourself. Don't compare yourself with others. Each of you must take responsibility for doing the creative best you can with your own life." Galatians 6:4-5

You have only one life to live, why would you want to spend it comparing yourself to someone else? There is absolutely nothing wrong with getting inspiration from the work of others or admiring how much they have accomplished, but the moment you start to compare your journey with theirs is when those thoughts turn toxic. We all have a specific assignment, mission or objective. Our assignments look different because they are meant to. God has already given each of us everything we need to accomplish the assignment without converting our names, gifts, talents or abilities. It's time for you to find freedom in who you are. You are anointed to accomplish your assignment.

WHAT HELPED ME:

- Identifying the purpose killers in my life.

- Taking the time to deal with each one.

- Getting a coach who helped me deal with areas I couldn't overcome on my own.

LET'S PAUSE AND REFLECT HERE

PURPOSE QUESTIONS:

Find a secluded area and take the time to write down the things that you have allowed to become an obstacle.

- How has the enemy tried to distract you from your purpose?

  _____

- Whose validation have you been seeking before stepping into your purpose?

  _____

- How have you been comparing your story to others?

  _____

PURPOSE ACTION:

- Find a secluded area and take the time to write down the things that you have identified as purpose killers in your own life. Don't hold back, it's time to get vulnerable because you cannot fix what you will not face.

Did you know that your purpose has an adversary? In 1 Peter 5:8 we read: *"Be sober [well balanced and self-disciplined], be alert and cautious at all times. That enemy of yours, the devil, prowls around like a roaring lion [fiercely hungry] seeking someone to devour."*

All these purpose killers have one thing in common, and that is to abort your purpose. It is an assignment focused on destroying your potential and leaving you directionless. The wonderful thing is that *"No weapon that is formed against you will succeed; And every tongue that rises against you in judgment you will condemn. This [peace, righteousness, security, and triumph over opposition] is the heritage of the servants of the Lord, and this is their vindication from Me,"* says the Lord. Isaiah 54:17

The weapon may form but it will not succeed!

CHAPTER 6

INFLUENCE AND IMPACT

CHAPTER 6

INFLUENCE AND IMPACT

EMPOWERED WOMEN EMPOWER THEIR WORLD

"Do not merely look out for your own

personal interests, but also f

or the interests of others."

Philippians 2:4

IT'S ABOUT THE ONE

You have felt it for a while now, that stirring in your heart that you are called to do something greater, but you are not sure what that is. You've been told you're good at certain things, you like doing certain things, but you have an inkling that you were made for more. But what is the more?

As one of five children and the only daughter of my parents, I grew up in a home that I can only describe as "Ein Gedi", an oasis. It was a place that people came to for advice, encouragement, help, refuge and even just for a weekend away from home. It wasn't the house itself that drew them to spending time in our home, it was be- cause of the people... my parents, Mike and Liz Richardson.

As a young girl, there were two things I knew I wanted to do when I grew up: I wanted to be a blessing to others and to make an impact in their lives. I saw my parents living this out on a daily basis and knew that it was what I wanted to mirror. Added to that, my parents had a remarkable way of making people feel like they belonged and to me it seemed like there was always room in their hearts and home for one more.

Even today they remain generous with their time and their space. They invest in people and this is testament to who they are and the legacy that they are building.

At the time I didn't realize it, but they had influence and they were making an impact, but most of all they were starting with the one. Because the one matters! I was witness to how individuals can bring light into the lives of others by just starting with one.

BE THE LIGHT

What does it mean to have influence and to truly make an impact?

Influence is doing everything God needs you to do. It's about being available, and being available doesn't mean it's always convenient.

It's not about accomplishment but rather about being a vessel and a voice.

But having a voice is not enough, you need to know how and when to use it. There is no doubt that the world needs what you have to offer. You. The person reading this.

Your impact might be vast and visible like Mother Teresa. Your im- pact might be quiet and profound like the unsung heroes we en- counter every single day who make humanity a little better. Either way, the world needs you. It's time to step up, speak up and do what you have been designed to do. You know that it's profoundly liberat- ing to not only know your purpose in life but to also know that your purpose is having an effect on people you know and maybe even some that you don't.

When we make the decision to use our influence for impact, we might come up against old limiting beliefs that whisper: "What dif- ference can I make – I'm only one person?" or "Who am I to change the world?"

Well, I'm going to stop you right there!

All that limiting beliefs do is cloud your vision, bury your purpose and make you feel like you couldn't possibly make a difference. I don't need to know you to know that these feelings will surface. You are human, after all, but the good news is that once we push through those limiting beliefs, we find out what our true purpose is. That is when you begin to learn to ignore the voice of doubt.

The story of Queen Esther in the Bible is a beautiful story. It's the story of a young orphan girl who was taken into the palace for twelve months of preparation before going before the King, who was look- ing for a new Queen. The story of Esther always stood out to me as a story of courage. Whenever I read it, I was always in awe of her bravery to stand before the King without being summoned. Proto- col was very important back then, and breaking the rules could lead to death, but Esther was willing to risk her own life for her people, without being certain of the outcome.

I am now struck by Esther's use of her influence, and how she used her voice to help others. In Esther 4:14, her uncle Mordecai says to her:

For if you remain completely silent at this time, relief and deliverance will arise for the Jews from another place, but you and your father's house will perish. Yet who knows whether you have come to the kingdom for such a time as this?

He challenged her to use her influence and her voice and the moment she did, she could bravely walk into the King's court without fear of persecution.

What will happen if you choose to remain silent? If you decide not to use your influence to bring change, not to use your voice to create impact? What will happen is that deliverance will come from another place.

If you refuse to take up space, and to walk in purpose, you are bound to drift aimlessly through precious days. Eventually this will become tiresome, frustrating and unrewarding.

When you walk into a dark room, the first thing you look for is the light and as you run your hand against the wall looking for the switch you start to wonder what you will find in the room. Will there be someone hiding in the shadows? Will you be surprised by what the room looks like? Will you like what you see? As soon as the light is switched on, it changes the way the room looks. The dark shadows that only a few seconds before, seemed so scary, don't seem so threatening anymore.

Here's the thing friend, you and I were created to be a light in the world. We are called to affect change in the lives of others and how do we do that? By being the light in a dark, and sometimes scary, world.

This is exactly what Esther did. She was walking into the unknown, but she decided to be the light that was needed and she allowed her light to shine. She was able to use her voice and influence with the King for the good of her people.

A few years ago, I sat in a church conference feeling uninspired. To be honest, I was feeling a little sorry for myself. I knew that I was pregnant with vision but for some reason I just couldn't break through to knowing exactly what that vision was. As I sat there, paging through my Bible, I came across Philippians 2:4. Now, I am certain that I had read this scripture before. I'm sure that I was even able to quote it given the chance. But on this particular day while sit- ting in a church conference, this verse was illuminated. I read it over and over and over again and even during the next couple of weeks leading into months I continued to not only read it but also meditate on it. It became a beacon of light in my own purpose journey. I began to sense God leading me in specific areas, making me aware of certain situations and calling me to not only help others but to be a light. It brought a childhood memory to mind: One of seeing how my parents were the light in the lives of so many people who need- ed it, of a young girl, whose only prayer was; "Lord, let people see Jesus in me and let me be a light."

Today, I continue to yearn to see this realized: That I would be a light to a world that needs it.

How about you?

In what "court" does your voice need to be heard? Where do you need to be an influence? Where do you need to make your light shine?

WHAT HELPED ME:

- Understanding that influence is about presence.

- Focusing my heart, time, energies and priorities to be impactful.

- Knowing that to have influence is to actively speak up. Influence doesn't require a platform; it only requires willingness.

- Learning that influence requires surrender. To surrender to my idea of how things should work out and trusting God to give direction.

LET'S PAUSE AND REFLECT HERE

_____

PURPOSE QUESTIONS:

- What issues in the world make you sad, happy or angry?

  _____

  _____

- How would you like to be remembered?

  _____

  _____

- What kind of life roles do you enjoy living out?

  _____

  _____

- What would a good friend say are your best attributes?

  _____

  _____

PURPOSE ACTION:

Take a moment to note one thing you can do today to influence the lives of others positively. Once you have done that one thing, find a second thing and continue.

Purpose is found in the doing, not in the thinking and that's why it's important to take action. Although you cannot see how it will all work out, we must have faith and seek God's plans, thoughts and strategies. Then, by trusting Him and faithfully walking it out, He will unlock the very best.

God knows the plan He has for our lives and His plan requires faith and obedience. You are filled with purpose. The world needs your voice, the world needs your love, the world needs you to be well in your soul. You are a world changer, destined for greatness!

"I don't speak because I have the power to speak; I speak because I don't have the power to remain silent." Rabbi A.Y.Kook

CHAPTER 7

PURPOSE DRIVEN LIVING

91

PURPOSE DRIVEN LIVING

ACTIVATE THE PROVERBS 31 WOMAN

"If you don't know what you're

living for, you haven't yet lived."

Rabbi Noah Weinberg

A SEASON OF REINVENTION

"I am tired of not progressing and not moving into what God has in store for me. Enough is enough!"

These were the words I wrote in my journal a few years ago. On the one hand, I was completely overwhelmed and at the same time I was underwhelmed. I was burnt out and tired, I was showing up for everyone but myself.

The restlessness and uncertainty left me feeling empty and directionless and to be honest, I was sad. I felt like my light had grown dim and I didn't know how to move from this place of being stuck. Now, don't misunderstand me, I was by no means unhappy with my life. I was unhappy with the feeling of knowing there was more, but not knowing how to pinpoint what that more looked like.

I knew that there was something specific that God was calling me to, but I didn't know how to make that move into my purpose. I strongly believed that there was a specific assignment I needed to move into, in order to birth a dream that was, as yet, unseen.

And then two things happened. I read Jeremiah 29:11: *"For I know the thoughts that I think toward you, says the LORD, thoughts of peace and not of evil, to give you a future and a hope."* When I say I read it, I mean I really read it and allowed the words to take root deep in my spirit.

It was then that I started to grasp that God already has a future and a hope in store for me and that I needed to figure out what that actually means.

The next thing I did was make the decision that I didn't want *"purpose driven living"* to just sound like a cute phrase, I wanted to really live a purpose driven life.

And what better way to figure all this out than to go to the Creator Himself and ask Him. I was born with a purpose to fulfill and I knew God didn't create anything without a purpose, so I needed to understand what that purpose was and its specific meaning for me.

And so I began my journey of reinvention!

Reinvention: the action or process through which something is changed.

To reinvent is to revive, reawaken, refresh, regenerate, restore or renew.

Now, this doesn't mean that I went on a quest to change who I was. I simply made a decision to discover who I was, what I was created to do, what I was passionate about and how to intentionally use my gifts and talents. Reinvention is not about changing who you are, it's about changing the things you do so that you can become the person you were always meant to be. It's about coming into alignment with the original intention for your life.

CONFIDENT FEMININITY

The next thing that happened was that I started to study the life of the Proverbs 31 woman, a woman of virtue as we have so often read and heard.

Raise your hand if, just like me, you have always felt intimidated when hearing or reading about this "wonder woman"!

Many women sigh in hesitation when they hear about her. Some women may even skip past this section. The mere mention of her conjures up an unrealistic image that instantly seems like a burden. A woman who seemed to have it all together. But before deciding to turn to the next chapter, let's really take a look into who this woman is.

She is an industrious housewife, a shrewd businesswoman, an enterprising trader, a generous benefactor and wise teacher. She excels at womanhood, wife-hood, motherhood and every other hood you can think of.

To be honest, I always felt overwhelmed and lacking when I thought of this seemingly perfect woman. And so I understand if you do too, trust me I really do. This is why I am so glad you opened this book, so don't avoid reading about her.

I want to help you change your perspective.

I want you to realize that reading about this woman is not so you can hold a mirror up to your own life and just see inadequacies.

The message of this woman is centered around three things:

- Her faith

- Her characteristics

- Her purpose

She is living out a life of purpose. She is not spending her days comparing herself to anyone else, or watching someone else's life. Instead she is living out her authentic self.

Before we dig a little deeper, let's get one thing straight: the Proverbs 31 woman is not the model of a perfect woman because we are not called to perfection. That woman doesn't exist. She is not real.

Now that we've cleared that up, let's go a little deeper into who this woman is.

If you look closely at Proverbs 31:10-31 you will see that this portion of scripture is a thirty-five-fold description of a woman split into the following sections:

- Her personal character and value

- Her husband's confidence

- Her ceaseless labours

- Her good works of charity

- Her household

- Her personal appearance

- Her husband's respect

- Her industry

- Her characteristics

- Her diligence

- Her praise and godliness

The opening verse of Proverbs 31 reads: "The words of King Lemuel, the prophecy that his mother taught him." Nothing else is found in scriptures concerning Lemuel aside from two mentions at the beginning of Proverbs 31. Jewish legend identifies him as Solomon, taking this advice from his mother Bathsheba. Should that be the case, this means that Bathsheba is the author of the inspired words of this section of Proverbs.

Who was Bathsheba?

She was the wife of Uriah the Hittite and later of David. She is most known for the biblical narrative in which she was summoned by King David, who had seen her bathing and lusted after her. She was the mother of Solomon who succeeded David as king, making her the Queen mother.

Bathsheba was by no means a perfect woman. We can clearly see that the main point of this passage is to show us the kind of character we can have as we fear and follow God. We might say that she is a strong woman, but her greatest strength lies in her wisdom, rooted in the fear of the Lord.

You can be a Proverbs 31 woman and more, but it doesn't mean that you do it all at the same time. The cycle of human life is portioned off into seasons and these seasons look different at each stage of life.

For example, if you are running your own business it is impossible to multitask perfectly while homeschooling four children, serving on various committees at your local church, run a soup kitchen in your community, keep your house spotless, mentor a group of young girls, make your husband have the best night of his life each and every evening, maintain a healthy lifestyle of exercise, all while cooking healthy nutritious meals from scratch, while making sure you make time for yourself and get enough sleep.

It is important to remember that understanding our purpose is much more of a discovery process than it is an instant download. It involves times of introspection and being real about the things that have been holding you back.

We often go around saying, *"I'm trying to find my purpose."* when in reality your purpose was never hiding from you. It was waiting for you to awaken to it. Sometimes we discount what our purpose is because it doesn't look like "Mary's" or "Suzie's" and its often not packaged in the way we would like.

What the Proverbs 31 woman shows me is my capabilities. That when I remain grounded in the word of God and His will for my life, I am capable of confidently walking in purpose. Don't look at the Proverbs 31 woman as everything you are not, see her as a woman completely sold out to her purpose, walking it out in the best way she can.

MAKE ROOM FOR GRACE

Something I also want you to know is that it takes more than just praying and reading your Bible. It also takes unearthing the things that no longer serve you, it takes committing to the decision to be authentically you, it takes commitment, consistency and having a workable plan.

I will say it again, purpose is not in the thinking, it is in the doing. It is in trying various things that will draw out your purpose.

With all that being said, if you are to fulfill your purpose within the greater plan for humanity, you need to commit to the process. In the same breath, you need to extend grace to yourself. You won't always get it right, there are times when you will require help. Know that it's okay to put down the "superwoman" cape and admit that you don't have everything under control. That cape you so valiantly try to hold on to just might be the snare that confines you.

You are called to a life of significance, a life that matters. To live in purpose is to live with intention. To take all the different pieces of your life, examine them and decide which of the pieces are holding you back, and which are the ones that will propel you forward.

Your purpose is a blueprint. This blueprint is a combination of the gifts, talents and the unique expression that makes you who you are. Purpose is when your gift, passion and calling come together for you to be of service to others. You know what it is when you discover who you are purposed to be. That is when you begin to see that significance.

A purpose driven life can look like many different things. It can look like:

- An ageing Grandmother who unexpectedly lost a daughter and now has to care for her grandkids.

- A teacher who wakes up every day to walk into a classroom to teach kids who do not respect her.

- A woman who takes her time and finances to feed hungry neighborhood kids every single day.

- A woman who prays for the needs of others.

- A woman who takes the time to invest in the lives of young people that society has labelled "not worth it".

- A woman who chooses to be a light in a world that so desperately needs it.

It's seeing a need and addressing it. It's knowing that you were called to make a difference.

If you want to step out of mediocrity and into purpose, you are going to have to say YES and be willing to do the work.

THINGS TO REMEMBER:

- You are God's idea. You are special and have been created as a solution to a problem.
- You have a purpose to fulfill.
- You have gifts, talents and abilities that you need to use to make an impact in the world.
- You have the potential to do great things, by simply being who you were created to be.
- Your uniqueness is a reflection of God's purpose and design for you.
- You have influence and it needs to be used to fulfil your individual assignment.

THESE ARE THE THINGS THAT HELPED ME:

- I asked for guidance. There is tremendous power in asking for help.

- I plugged into a community of heart minded women.

- I decided to pursue what sets my heart on fire.

It's your turn to pause and reflect on how you can learn from the attributes of the Proverbs 31 woman.

LET'S PAUSE AND REFLECT HERE

PURPOSE QUESTIONS:

- What makes you feel confident?

  _____

  _____

- Who are the people that naturally gravitate towards you?

  _____

  _____

- Why do people come to you for this specific thing?

  _____

  _____

- What would happen if you dropped the impostor syndrome and just served?

  _____

  _____

- How are people changed or transformed as a result of what you do for them?

  _____

  _____

- How are they better for having been in contact with you?

_____

_____

PURPOSE ACTION:

Write down 10 things that make you unique.

1._____

2._____

3._____

4._____

5._____

6._____

7._____

8._____

9._____

10._____

One of my favorite scriptures is Ephesians 2:10 that says, _"For we are His workmanship, created in Christ Jesus for good works, which God prepared beforehand, that we should walk in them."_

God has already gone before you in creating the works for you to do. The key is to get in alignment with where He is leading you, and to do it with confidence, joy and in the knowledge, that you are uniquely you.

CHAPTER 8

PURPOSE IN RELATIONSHIPS

CHAPTER 8

PURPOSE IN RELATIONSHIPS

DESTINY CONNECTIONS

"If there ever comes a time when the women of the world
come together purely and simply for the benefit

of mankind, it will be a force such as the

world has never known."

Matthew Arnold

COMMUNITY OVER COMPETITION

I once heard a story about female elephants. In the wild, when a mama elephant is giving birth, all the other female elephants in the herd back around her in formation. They close ranks so the delivering mama cannot ever be seen in the middle. They stomp and kick up dirt and soil to throw attackers off the scent and basically act like a pack of fierce bodyguards.

They surround the mama and incoming baby in protection, sending a clear signal to predators that if they want to attack their friend while she is vulnerable, they'll have to get through forty tons of female aggression first.

When the baby elephant is delivered, the sister elephants do two things: they kick sand or dirt over the newborn to protect its fragile skin from the sun and then they all start trumpeting. A female celebration of new life, of sisterhood, of something beautiful being born in a harsh, wild world despite enemies and attackers and predators and odds.

Girls, this is exactly what we are supposed to do for one another. When our sisters are vulnerable, when they are giving birth to new life, new ideas, new ministries, new businesses and new spaces. When they are under attack, when they need their circle to surround them so they can create, deliver, heal, recover, we get into formation. We close ranks and literally have each other's backs. We do the heavy lifting while our sister is down. You want to mess with our girl? Come through us first! And when delivery comes, when new life makes its entrance, when healing begins, when the night has passed and our sister is ready to rise back up, we sound our trumpets because we saw it through together. We celebrate! We cheer! We raise our voices and give thanks.

There is nothing like being surrounded by women who will go to war for you. It is an honour to be part of a God-given community of women that has triumphed together in every generation since the beginning of time.

Maybe you need to be reminded of the importance of sisterhood, of closing ranks around a vulnerable sister, or if your girls have you surrounded while you are tender, this is how we do it. We take turns in the middle. We take turns in formation. We take turns being vulnerable. We take turns being strong.

What is powerful to me about this story, is that it is only through the herd of elephants' collaborative effort, only through their fierce loyalty to the group and only through the courage of each elephant to support the TRIBE in times of trouble, that they succeed! What is great about the power of collaboration exemplified in the story, is that it breeds LIFE and CELEBRATION and GRATITUDE!

There is no community like a community of women. We are the crown of creation and together we are magic! The questions is… who are you spending your time with?

Jim Rohn says: "You are the average of the five people you spend the most time with."

Who are your people? Is it people who encourage you, surround you and build you up or those who speak negatively and pull you down?

How do you feel after being in the presence of these people? Do you feel upbeat, encouraged and positive or broken down, hopeless and discouraged?

It may sound like a cliché, but it really does matter who you spend your time with. It really does matter who is in your corner.

The disciples hung around Jesus. Why do you think that is? Could it be because He spoke truth into their lives, because He encouraged them while challenging them at the same time? Or was it because He gave them purpose and direction? Aside from the disciples, there were people who followed Jesus for miles and even days. Jesus was all for community!

Relational alignments are critical to living the life God intends for you. It is said, "If you want to go fast in life, go alone, but if you want to go far, go with people." But not just with any people, the right kind of people.

We were made to be in community. Yes, people will let you down, they will disappoint you and you are likely to do the same to them, but there is something to be said about the gift of community. The gift of having someone you can turn to and lean on. Some of us need just one person and some of us need a tribe. But we all need community!

SETTING HER UP TO WIN

The book of Ruth is a great example of a destiny connection. It relates that Ruth and Orpah, two women of Moab, had married two sons of Elimelech and Naomi, Judeans who had settled in Moab to escape a famine in Judah. The husbands of all three women die and Naomi plans to return to her native Bethlehem and urges her daughters-in law to return to their families. Orpah does so, but Ruth refuses to leave Naomi declaring in Ruth 1:16-17: "Do not urge me to leave you or to turn back from following you; for where you go, I will go, and where you lodge, I will lodge. Your people will be my people, and your God my God. Where you die, I will die, and there I will be buried. May the Lord do the same to me [as He has done for you], and more also, if anything but death separates me from you."

Ruth accompanies Naomi to Bethlehem and later marries Boaz, a distant relative of her late father-in-law. She is a symbol of abiding loyalty and devotion to another woman. Despite dealing with her own heartache and trauma she chose to remain faithful to the relationship she and Naomi had built. Later in the book of Ruth, we are able to see how, in turn, Naomi was able to bring advice exactly when Ruth needed it.

This is proof that when women speak life into the lives of other women, miracles happen!

I believe that God intentionally puts people on our paths who will cause a lasting and tangible impact, shifting the trajectories of our lives forever. The question is, will you recognize them when they show up?

There has long been a narrative that women don't support one another, and it is misleading and damaging to our relationships. It fuels the fire of perfectionism and plants seeds of self-doubt, comparison and competition.

Really, at our core, we all want the same things. We want a life that we love, and this is what ties us all together. Our methods may look different but at the end of it all we don't need more standards to be measured up against, we need support.

Ann Voskamp says: "I won't judge you for dishes in your sink and shoes all over your floor and laundry on your couch. I won't judge you for choosing not to spend your one life weeding the garden or washing the windows or working on organizing the pantry. I won't judge you for the size of your waist, the flatness, bigness, cut or color of your hair, the hipness or the matronliness of your clothes, and I won't judge whether you work at a stove, a screen, a store, a steering wheel, a sink or a stage. I won't judge you for where you are on your road, won't belittle your offering, your creativity, your battle, your work. "

Amen to that!

Let's deliberately stop the judgment that seems to be a tell-tale signature of so-called femininity. We all have a different journey and each of us is uniquely equipped to carry it out. When we sit next to another woman with that frame of mind we begin to appreciate our differences, and are better able to champion each other.

THINGS THAT HELPED ME DISCOVER MY TRIBE:

- I did an audit on my circle. This is not an easy process but a necessary one.

- I became intentional about surrounding myself with those who have a heart to see me thrive. In return I was able to bring the same genuine heart to my sister circle.

- I prayed for discernment in knowing who was for me and who wasn't.

Take some time to reflect on your own relationships.

LET'S PAUSE AND REFLECT HERE

PURPOSE QUESTIONS:

- Are you in relationships that are in alignment with your purpose?

  _____

- Are the women in your circle building you up or bringing you down?

  _____

- Are your conversations toxic or life-giving?

  _____

- How do you feel after spending time with them?

  _____

- Are you setting them up to win with them doing the same for you?

  _____

PURPOSE ACTION:

Avail yourself to be a support to someone who needs it.

As iron sharpens iron, so a friend sharpens a friend. Proverbs 27:17 May you be a woman who sharpens another and realizes the beauty of sisterhood in all its forms.

CHAPTER 9

PURPOSE IN ENTREPRENEURSHIP

PURPOSE IN ENTREPRENEURSHIP

PURSUE PURPOSE NOT MONEY

"If your dreams do not scare you,

they are not big enough."

Ellen Johnson Sirleaf

WORTH THE RISK

I finally decided to do it. I was going to resign from my corporate job and start a business. I didn't want to be old and grey one day sitting on a comfy chair saying: "I could have, I should have, but I didn't" For as long as I could remember that was the plan, and the time had finally come.

The idea alone had me on a euphoric high. I was finally taking the step into entrepreneurship and the thought exhilarated me as much as it scared me. I put all my plans in place, resigned from my job and then I was alone.

I worked extremely hard to get everything in place while I prepared to officially launch and then one day, just before the launch I received a message from someone who, in my mind, supported the vision and was cheering me on from the sidelines. The message said that I was making a mistake, that my launch would be unsuccessful as people would not support an unknown speaker at an unknown event with an unknown entrepreneur.

I was gutted!

Those words echoed loudly over the next few days and had me wondering… "Can I really do this?"

Thankfully I already had a strong support system who were eagerly waiting to witness the next chapter of my life and I remembered that this vision that had been ignited in my heart is not man-given it is God-given. The Creator, Himself had placed a desire in my heart to be effective and influential in the marketplace. How dare I question His gift on my life simply because someone else thought otherwise.

The truth is that not everyone is going to understand your vision, and that's okay because they are not supposed to. You are the one that is meant to see it, believe in it and work towards it. Their opinion is not required!

Zig Ziglar writes: "It would be "safer" for a ship to stay in the harbor, "safer" for a plan to stay on the ground and "safer" for a house to remain empty, because a ship encounters "risk" when it leaves the harbor, a plane encounters "risk" when it leaves the ground and a house invites "risk" when someone moves in. But the ship would collect barnacles and become unseaworthy even faster in the harbor. A plane would rust much faster on the ground, and the house would deteriorate much faster standing empty."

Starting a business is exciting, it is an opportunity to step into something unknown and it is filled with risk. You risk not knowing the outcome, you risk trying something and failing, you even risk loss, but worse than the risk is never knowing if it would have worked out. Sure, you'll be uncomfortable. Every entrepreneur is a beginner and starts off uncertain. You just need to commit to making it happen, to taking the first step and trusting that you'll figure out how to take the second step when you need to do so.

KNOW WHO YOU ARE SERVING

Fulfillment comes from seeing the impact your purpose has on others but we have to be careful of making the mistake in thinking that what we have to offer is for everyone.

You might say things like:

- I want everyone to try this and see how good it is.

- I want everyone to feel empowered.

- I want everyone to overcome trauma and have a healthy self- esteem.

- I want everyone to experience the joy of using my product.

As noble as this sounds, it is not practical. People need to know that they are the ones you are talking to. If you are not for someone specific, then what you offer will be for no one. When you talk to everyone the exact same way, you alienate people and no one resonates with your message.

Clarity comes in knowing who you serve before you can understand how to serve them but most of all, clarity comes from knowing your why.

Saying that you serve women is too broad a statement. Who is this woman? What pain point does this woman have that you are trying to solve? How will you use your gift and expertise to support her?

When I remembered that I was a solution to a problem, the words of the naysayers didn't matter anymore.

A few tips for figuring out who are you serving in your business:

- Who do you naturally enjoy being around?
- What types of people do you naturally enjoy supporting?
- What in your history, background or training makes you relatable to the person you want to serve?
- Who are you talking to?

Don't feel bad for not talking to everyone. Serve those you are called to serve.

The clearer you become on who your people are, the easier it will be to find them and that's how you'll know how to serve them. Once you know how to serve them your purpose is clear.

IDENTIFY YOUR WHY

Being an entrepreneur means that you are someone who identifies a problem, and comes up with a solution for monetary gain, but you also need to know why you do what you do.

Simon Sinek shares a brilliant idea that has transformed how businesses market their products and services. He says, "People don't buy what you do. They buy why you do it."

Do you know what your "why" is and are you clear on how to communicate that why?

Things that helped me get to my why:

- Understanding my gift. The thing I do better than anyone else around me, and with the least amount of effort.
- Giving myself permission to be passionate about the gift, to embrace the gift, to acknowledge it and not doubt it.
- Merging the gift with the passion and taking the steps to move forward in action.

EMBRACE YOUR CAPABILITIES

What makes me think I can do it? Does that sound familiar?

You think you are not qualified to serve your people, so you don't. You have always wanted to start a business but think you need a bus load of degrees and a ton of experience before you get started. You feel like a fraud for even thinking you can be successful and grow a sustainable business. You feel like an impostor!

Imposter syndrome is defined as: The persistent inability to believe that one's success is deserved or has been legitimately achieved as a result of one's own efforts or skills.

A pervasive feeling of self-doubt, insecurity, or fraudulence despite often overwhelming evidence to the contrary.

Impostor syndrome manifests itself especially in entrepreneurship. You feel like a fake, or that you are appealing to luck which results in minimizing accomplishments.

The Bible tells us: "We are destroying sophisticated arguments and every exalted and proud thing that sets itself up against the [true] knowledge of God, and we are taking every thought and purpose captive to the obedience of Christ." 2 Corinthians 10:5

As we covered in the chapter on Mindset, it is important to be aware of what you are thinking about, especially when it does not line up with what the word of God says.

Being aware of your gifts is, in itself, a competitive advantage. The gifts given to you are free and are meant to be used, it's time to take the bow off and get to work. When you begin to question the gift you begin to walk in uncertainty and open yourself up to the lies saying you are not good enough. They tell you that you are pretending to be something you are not. Imagine how God feels knowing that He has given you these free gifts to make an impact in your world, and you have taken them and put them aside to chase something that He has not called you to do.

What would it look like if you put down the mantle of inadequacy and instead chose to rise up and embrace everything that is already inside of you?

I can tell you what would happen, you would do great things!

Now there are two areas of entrepreneurship that I have found women hesitant to talk about: Marketing and Money.

MARKETING

You are scared to sell!

You feel that if you market and promote what you are doing, you are in some way boasting. I understand, I've been there myself. We get so caught up in being humble that it's no longer humility but self- depreciation. And how is God glorified in this?

You need to empower yourself with a dose of confidence. This confidence comes in knowing that I am well equipped to drive this business, that God has gifted me with the ability to do certain things for the good of others and His glory.

Think about it. If you have identified a problem and you have the solution to that problem, it becomes your responsibility to offer it up to the world.

If you are in the marketplace and have what people need but don't offer it:

1. You leave them suffering.
2. You waste your time.

The offer you are making to them is an offer to serve and sales is service but how will they know what you have to offer if you don't tell them?

Effective marketing is simple, it's about great communication.

FIVE KEY THINGS YOU NEED TO KNOW WHEN MARKETING:

1. Who you are.
2. Who your customers are.
3. Where they are and how you find them.
4. How to talk to them.
5. How to communicate what you have to offer.

Once you have figured this out, get out there and start talking to the right people in the right way. If you have something great to offer, then you need to be confident enough to share it with the world.

MONEY

"And you shall remember the Lord your God, for it is He who gives you power to get wealth, that He may establish His covenant which He swore to your fathers, as it is this day." Deuteronomy 8:18

I believe in pursuing purpose, not money and I definitely believe in people over profit. Sometimes the problem is not someone's ability to make money but their belief about making money. The verse above clearly states that it is God who gives us the power to get wealth, so that His covenant may be established. If He has given you the ability, why do you have trouble receiving it?

If you want to run a business, then you will have to treat it as such. There is a difference between a business and a hobby: a business makes you money and a hobby costs you money. If you are providing a service or selling a product that means you need to charge for it. Yes, you may say "I don't care about the money" or "I do it because I love it" and that is perfectly fine but then you are not in business.

If your business is not earning you an income, then it's difficult to justify calling it one.

Rabbi Daniel Lapin says, *"Few people can truly excel at occupations about which they entertain moral reservations."*

If you feel guilty for making money, being successful or winning at something this is a limiting belief that will hinder you from making money, being successful or winning.

Some other limiting beliefs you may have:

- **Making money is immoral:** Making money is good. It's not about greed or taking advantage of others. It is a resource that allows us to accomplish the things we need to.

- **Money is evil:** The Bible says the love of money (that is, the greedy desire for it and the willingness to gain it unethically) is a root of all sorts of evil, and some by longing for it have wandered away from the faith and pierced themselves (through and through) with many sorrows. 1 Timothy 6:10

- **Running a business ethically for full payment constitutes greed:** Money is a necessary resource. Almost everything in life requires money. Want to get married? Weddings cost money. Want to have children? They cost a lot. Want to buy gifts or give to charity. It requires money.

Living in abundance means that you are also able to freely sow into the lives of others. You are able to meet needs wherever God leads you. You are able to provide for every good cause and you need to make an income for that to happen, your business needs to make money.

We are called to stewardship and to do this, you will need something to steward.

THINGS THAT HELPED ME IN STARTING A BUSINESS:

- I did my research to make sure I knew what I was getting into.

- I made a plan and created goals in order to carry out that plan.

- I sought advice about the things I didn't know.

- I built collaborative relationships with other entrepreneurs.

Here are a few things to get you thinking or to help you gain clarity.

PURPOSE QUESTIONS:

- What would it look like if you picked up your gift and used it to make an impact and an income?

  _____

- What is the pain, frustration or challenge that the people you are called to serve have, and how will you serve them?

  _____

- How will you not only make impact but income?

  _____

- What are the limiting beliefs you have around money?

  _____

- What reasons have you made up about not being able to sell or make an offer in the marketplace?

  _____

PURPOSE ACTION:

Think about how you can serve others well in business.

On your entrepreneurial journey, you will experience seasons of preparation, negotiating, insignificance, tears, disappointment, chaos and also great joy and plenty. If you are passionate about entrepreneurship, gifted at a craft, and have been given opportunities to use those gifts to love and serve others, you are called to create. Now it is your responsibility to steward those God-given abilities well, so that one day you may hear the words, *"Well done, good and faithful servant."*

CHAPTER 10
PERSONAL DEVELOPMENT

PERSONAL

DEVELOPMENT

LIFELONG LEARNER

"An investment in knowledge

pays the best interest."

Benjamin Franklin

INVEST IN YOU

Now that you have all this information about identity, discovering your gifts and talents, your passion, building authentic relationships, influencing your world and ultimately living in purpose, what do you do now?

That is simple enough to answer. Now you invest in yourself!

It takes intention and sometimes support to see the pattern between who you were created to be, what you were purposed to do, doing what you love and fitting it into a model specifically designed for your life.

In the chapter on gifts and talents, I wrote about my aversion for public speaking that resulted from being constantly told that I talk too much. As a result, I carried that label for a very long time. Anytime I got asked to be a programme director, to speak on a certain topic or do anything that required me to use my voice I literally froze. The thought alone would bring me such apprehension that I would feel sick to my stomach. Something that God had gifted me to do became almost like a noose around my neck.

This was until one day when I made a decision. I decided that I was going to take action, that this thing that I dislike so much, this thing that filled me with so much dread would no longer be allowed to have a hold on me.

I was going to take control of it and see where it led me.

I decided to invest in developing and nurturing this gift. I enrolled for courses, I attended webinars and workshops, I listened to podcasts and read books. All of this was in an effort to invest in something that I came to realize was a gift and that I had ignored for far too long. What happened is that in the year I decided to invest in myself, I got an opportunity to use that gift on thirteen different platforms. None of these opportunities were planned for. What I want you to know is that the moment I decided to embrace my gift, God began to open doors and His plan for my life began to unfold. And this is not exclusive to me, it can happen for you too.

BE WILLING TO DO THE WORK

So, what exactly is personal development and how do you implement it into your life? I am so glad you asked.

Personal development covers activities that improve awareness and identity, develop talents and potential, build human capital and facilitate employability, enhance the quality of life and contribute to the realization of dreams and aspirations. Personal development takes place over the course of a person's entire life.

In its simplest form, personal development is about self-improvement. It's finding out what areas you need to improve in yourself, and how are you going to improve them to ensure that you grow. It is the process of improving yourself through activities that bring about growth.

I see it as taking personal initiative for your future.

Personal development is an ongoing process of improvement either in your career, your education, your personal life, your business, your spiritual life or in all of these areas. It's about setting goals and putting plans in place to achieve those goals.

In order to experience personal growth in any area of your life, you must take some of your time and money to invest in acquiring knowledge and gaining wisdom. This investment will bear fruit and multiply your prospects of success not only in your chosen endeavor but in your life as a whole. This decision requires commitment and consistency. It requires that you show up, and are willing to do the work.

SIX SIMPLE WAYS TO BEGIN YOUR PERSONAL DEVELOPMENT JOURNEY:

1. **Develop a growth mindset.** Before you begin the work that is necessary for change, you have to believe that change is possible. The first place to start is by nurturing a growth mindset. Accept your potential and be willing to see it realized.
2. **Read, read and read.** I strongly believe in the saying: "Leaders are readers." Exposing yourself to authors

who write on the subject of your own personal improvement area is one of the most effective ways to move in the direction of your development.

3. **Listen to podcasts.** There are literally thousands of Podcasts covering just about every focus area of life that you can imagine, and guess what? They are completely free to download and listen to!

4. **Be proactive.** You could wait for change to come to you, or you could go out there and make it happen. Take the initiative.

5. **Draw out a detailed personal development plan.** This will help you know where you are headed and how to get there, focusing on specifics too.

6. **Seek out a coach or mentor.** A mentor is someone who will help you discover your areas for development and will have a heart to help you through the process. A coach will give you a plan and structure: Your own personalized strategy for success.

THINGS THAT HELPED ME:

- I committed to my growth in a specific area.

- I took personal responsibility and mapped out a plan for what my steps would be.

- I took the initiative to find the right resources and invest my time, money and energy in them.

- I read books on the specific area I wanted to work on and it helped me gain perspective. Jim Rohn says: "Reading is essential for those who seek to rise above the ordinary."

- I invested in a coach. The truth is we don't know what we don't know. And investing in someone who does know speeds up the learning process.

- I attended webinars and seminars that equipped me with the tools I needed.

LET'S PAUSE AND REFLECT HERE

PURPOSE QUESTIONS:

- Who has what you need?

  _____

- Who knows what you need to know and who has succeeded in the area of your calling?

  _____

- How can you leverage their experience to your advantage?

  _____

- How will you invest in your yourself and your dreams?

  _____

PURPOSE ACTION:

Decide on one area in which you would like to see growth. List all the things you need to do to make that happen.

I believe that personal development is one of the best investments you will ever make. Once you have an idea of the area you want to see grow, you need to brainstorm; this allows your creativity to flow. You need to do your research so that you have the knowledge to proceed and then you need to take action as this will bring you progress.

One of the most amazing aspects about personal development is the different ways it allows you to sow into the lives of others. I strongly believe in gaining knowledge but on its own it is not enough. You need to have the wisdom to use that knowledge on the right platforms and in the right way.

Follow in the footsteps of Jesus who, as a child, was found in the Temple in discussion with the elders. Even as a child He knew the value of being in a place of learning. Like Jesus, may you grow in wisdom and stature, and in favor with God and men.

FINAL THOUGHTS

Congratulations! If you have followed the purpose steps in each chapter, you now have a clear roadmap to fulfilling your God-given purpose.

Remember that purpose is found in the doing, you must take action. You have the tools and now you need to put them to work.

There is no need to do it all at once. If you do, you are bound to get overwhelmed and quit before you even start. Just start at the beginning, take a deep breath, and take one step at a time. Acknowledge that everything in life is a process, so embrace it.

Friend, don't become discouraged in the delays and allow them to make you give up on pursuing your purpose. Trust the process. The process is the place where you develop so that God's plan in your life can be realized.

I love cheering women on to pursue purpose, but you have to believe that you can and you will accomplish all that you have been called to.

You have gifts and passions for a reason, and I want to encourage you to use them.

Use them to make a difference in the lives of the people waiting on you.

Use them to influence and impact your sphere of the world. Use them to live a life of significance and abundance.

But most of all, use them for the glory of God and the good of others.

Dig your heels in, put the things we've talked about into practice, take on your assignment with everything you've got. It's time to lean into the purpose that is calling you and not the resistance holding you back. God is calling you, equipping you and preparing you according to His purpose within you.

I know you've got this and I'm cheering you on, every step of the way. So get out there and remember that you were born on purpose, for purpose, in purpose for such a time as this!

"Many are the plans in a person's heart, but it is the Lord's purpose that prevails." Proverbs 19:21

NOTES

INTRODUCTION

Jeremiah 29:11, AMP.

CHAPTER 1

Psalms 139:13-16.

Genesis 1:27, AMP.

CHAPTER 2

Romans 12:6-8 AMP.

CHAPTER 3

Inc, Startup Life, February 28,2018.

http://www.inc.com/peter-economy/this-is-way-you-need-to-write- down-your-goals-for-faster-success.html

Seth Godin, "On Owning It," October 30, 2013, http://sethgodin. typepad.com/seths_blog/2013/10/on-owning-it.html

Proverbs 13:19, NLT.

Ephesians 3:20, TPT.

CHAPTER 4

Caroline Leaf, Switch on your brain, BakerBooks, 2013
Ephesians 4:23, AMP.

Roger Bannister, https://www.history.com/.amp/this-day-in-history/ first-four-minute-mile

Cordia Harrington story, Christy Wright, Business Boutique, Ramsey Press, 2017

Philippians 4:8, AMP.

CHAPTER 5

James Clear, "How to focus and concentrate better," https://amesclear.com/howtofocus

https://biographics.org/viktor-frankl-biography-life-search-meaning/ Galatians 6:4-5, MSG.

1. Peter 5:8, AMP.

Isaiah 54:17, AMP.

Galatians 1:10, AMP.

CHAPTER 6

Esther 4:14, NKJV.

Philippians 2:4, AMP.

CHAPTER 7

Jeremiah 29:11, NKJV.

Ephesians 2:10, NKJV.

CHAPTER 8

Ruth 1:16-17, AMP

Proverbs 27:17, NLT

Ann Voskamp, "How Women Can Stop Judging Each Other: A Movement of Key Women," July 30, 2014,

http://www.aholyexperience.com/2014/07

CHAPTER 9

Zig Ziglar, See you at the top, Pelican Publishing, 1982

Simon Sinek, "How Great Leaders Inspire Action," TEDxPuget Sound, Filmed September 2009, https://www.ted.com/talks/simon_ sinek_how_great_leaders_inspire_action?language=en.

Deuteronomy 8:18, NKJV.

 1 Corinthians 10:5, AMP.

1 Timothy 6:10, AMP.

Rabbi Daniel Lapin, Thou Shall Prosper: Ten Commandments for Making Money, Wiley, 2009).

CHAPTER 10

https://en.m.wikipedia.org/wiki/personal_development

EPILOGUE

Proverbs 19:21, NIV.

www.ingramcontent.com/pod-product-compliance
Lightning Source LLC
Chambersburg PA
CBHW030837090426
42737CB00009B/1007

9 780620 911467